MODIGLIANI

MODIGLIANI

Laurent Seksik

*Translated from the French
by Joel Anderson and Stéfane Houssier*

PRESS LIMITED

First published in the United Kingdom in 2016 by
Salammbo Press
39A Belsize Avenue
London NW3 4BN

www.salammbopress.com

Copyright © 2016 Laurent Seksik

This English translation copyright © Salammbo Press 2016

The moral right of Laurent Seksik to be identified as the author of this work has been asserted in accordance with the Copyright, Designs and Patents Act 1988

All rights reserved. No part of this publication may be reproduced, distributed, or transmitted in any form or by any means, including photocopying, recording, or other electronic or mechanical methods, without the prior written permission of the publisher.

A CIP catalogue record for this book is available from the British Library.

Cover art by Fabrice Le Hénanff
Typeset by Tetragon, London

ISBN 978-0-9932344-1-5

CHARACTERS

AMEDEO MODIGLIANI (nickname Modi)

JEANNE HÉBUTERNE

ZBOROWSKI (nickname Zbo)

EUDOXIE, the mother of Jeanne

EUGÉNIE, the mother of Amedeo Modigliani

ACT ONE

A high ceilinged room, nearly empty, occupied by an easel, a table laid with brushes and palettes. In the back wall, a little to the right, a closed door (leading to a bedroom). Two chairs. Against the wall, canvases are stacked one in front of another. The place is quite messy. An empty bottle on the floor.

SCENE 1

A mother EUDOXIE HÉBUTERNE *and her daughter* JEANNE *in the studio.*

EUDOXIE: I don't understand how you can live here!
JEANNE: Because it's my home, Mother!
EUDOXIE: Your home, this room!?
JEANNE: There is also a bedroom.
EUDOXIE: A mattress on the floor… you had a proper room at home.
JEANNE: Now, I have my own.
EUDOXIE *(bends down, picks up the empty bottle)*: Not a cupboard. Not a table… do you even have enough to eat? You would tell me, Jeannette?
JEANNE: I would tell you, Mother.
EUDOXIE: So, why didn't you tell us that you were living with this man? Why did you lie?

JEANNE: You know perfectly well why... Father would have forbid me to see him. Or André would have locked me up.

EUDOXIE: Jeannette, you are talking about your brother left at the front, in the trenches... and then... why bother to lecture you? You have changed so much.

JEANNE: I haven't noticed anything.

EUDOXIE: Where did you learn to speak like this? We brought you up to respect and love God. We gave you French, dance, piano and art classes... perhaps you should have had classes in good manners?... But how can you live in this... mess?!

JEANNE: At the beginning, with Father, didn't you live in a precarious situation?

EUDOXIE: We perhaps did live in a precarious situation, but I'll say, if it means anything to you, we never lived in sin... and as far as I know, sin is not something you do temporarily... even at eighteen years old...

JEANNE: Nineteen!

EUDOXIE *(without noticing)*: To think... you could have had the world at your feet!... And here you are, on your knees before the worst of men!...

JEANNE: I'm not on my knees and he is the finest man on earth!

EUDOXIE: In his circle of drunks and failed artists?

JEANNE: One day, Mother, you will understand.

EUDOXIE: When the cows come home and the rats of Paris invade your room... Oh, I can't imagine, you, my little girl, so sweet, so precious, on... on... that mattress...

JEANNE: Mother!

EUDOXIE: We trusted you, Jeanne. We bowed to all your wishes. We agreed for you to enrol in the painting academy, as if that was any place for a young lady... as if a woman could become a painter! And this is how you thank us... you betray us, Jeanne. You betray who we are, what we believe in, our dreams, our expectations, all that our lives were. In the name of what, Jeannette?

JEANNE: In the name of my life.

EUDOXIE: A bohemian life with a depraved person...

JEANNE: You see, Mother, I learned from you something which remains close to my heart.

EUDOXIE *(looking around)*: I don't see anything here we have given to you.

JEANNE: Faith, Mother, your unwavering faith. The faith that makes you bless God before every meal, pray before sleeping, and cry in the church on Ash Wednesday.

EUDOXIE: Have you kept your faith!?

JEANNE: An immense faith, Mother... and I have faith in this man.

EUDOXIE: Is my little girl speaking like this?

JEANNE: I'm not a little girl any more, Mother.

EUDOXIE: And that's what young women aspire to? Living in slums with crazy men!

JEANNE: This is not a slum and Dedo is not crazy.

EUDOXIE *(as if to herself)*: I know I haven't been a perfect mother. I might have made mistakes... but this is unbearable.

JEANNE: What's unbearable?

EUDOXIE *(she picks up an empty sardine tin from the floor)*: This, Jeanne, this is unbearable.

JEANNE: Did you come to do the housework or to lecture me?

EUDOXIE: Jeanne, I want to bring you back to your senses.

JEANNE: No, Mother, you want to bring me back to your house!

EUDOXIE: If only I could…

JEANNE: Don't you understand? I want to live here… Here, I'm happy, I love and I'm loved.

EUDOXIE: Love… you think you know about love…? Where would you have learned about that?

JEANNE *(ironic)*: At home, perhaps, seeing you with Father…?

EUDOXIE: Mind how you speak to your mother, Jeanne! Even if you don't respect anything any more, neither cleanliness, nor your dignity, you should still respect your mother…

JEANNE *(keeping her head down)*: Forgive me.

EUDOXIE *(stroking Jeanne's cheek)*: I forgive you, Jeannette, my splendid little girl… look, even your face has changed. Before… *(She indicates the corner of Jeanne's lips.)* Here, I always found a little smile. A sign of affection, oh, I imagine it was not for me… but it was as if something within pleased you.

JEANNE: It's some*one* now, and you know his name… As for the corners of my mouth, if I may… I noticed that when I smiled, you would leave me alone. You stopped asking what was wrong with me, why I was so sad, telling me I should go outside for a while... Sorry, Mother, what you liked most wasn't really me!

EUDOXIE: I love you as you are.

JEANNE: And with whoever I want to be with?

EUDOXIE: Be with whoever you want!... But before I go, I would like to ask you a question.

JEANNE: Ask and I'll decide.

EUDOXIE: Jeanne, would you tell me if... you had some bad luck?

JEANNE: Why would you want bad luck to happen to me?

EUDOXIE: Understand what I'm saying! Do I need to say more!?... You know, it happens by accident. Snap, the beautiful girl finds herself with a bun in the oven...

JEANNE: Don't be vulgar!

EUDOXIE: You think he'll stay charming then, your Italian dandy? Think he'll burden himself with a woman with a big belly? You think he has a paternal instinct, your Modigliani? Animal instinct, more like...

JEANNE: Mother!

EUDOXIE: As soon as he hears the news, he'll run. He'll go back to chasing the girls of Montmartre, he'll search for fresh flesh and drown Jeanne Hébuterne's bump in alcohol.

JEANNE: You go too far!

EUDOXIE *(after a while)*: You will tell me if an accident happens, won't you?... Promise me... If I find out soon enough... I know people whose job it is to... who do that very well... some women, very cleanly...

JEANNE: And then?

EUDOXIE: Everything will go back to how it used to be.
JEANNE: Nothing will go back to how it used to be, Mother.
EUDOXIE: Yes it will! You'll understand exactly who this man is. You'll come back home.
JEANNE: Mother, you would put your daughter in the hands of some butchers, backstreet abortionists!?... No, I won't tell you anything.
EUDOXIE: You'll lie! Again! To your father and to me!
JEANNE: It's nearly six months since Father disowned me.
EUDOXIE *(more softly)*: I'm trying to convince him to see you again, to reopen that door. But it's not so easy... He had so much hope for his daughter. He loved you so much.
JEANNE: Loved me?...
EUDOXIE: And so to see his little Jeanne... with this depraved man. This...
JEANNE: This what!?
EUDOXIE: You know perfectly well what I'm talking about.
JEANNE: This wop?
EUDOXIE: If only that was it!
JEANNE: He's allowed to drink, isn't he?
EUDOXIE: Yes, you can be cured of such things.
JEANNE: But it is a hereditary defect, isn't it?
EUDOXIE: You know well that I have nothing against these people... I had a friend, well... an acquaintance, at school, Henriette Lévy, I had nothing against her.
EUDOXIE: What greatness of soul!
EUDOXIE: During the Dreyfus case, there weren't too many of us.
JEANNE: Those were the days...

SCENE 2

MODIGLIANI enters the room, holding a newspaper in his hand.

MODI *(exclaiming)*: O tempora, O mores! Ah, the queen mother! To what do we owe this honour?

EUDOXIE: I'm only passing by.

MODI: Well, pass then…

EUDOXIE: This is a gracious welcome, worthy of the finest of men.

MODI: But you can stay if you wish. Jeanne will be delighted. And as for me…

EUDOXIE: You?

MODI: Me! Do you care?

EUDOXIE: Tell me, we'll see.

MODI: I'll leave.

EUDOXIE: Stay, you're in your own house… Goodbye, my daughter.

JEANNE: Goodbye, Mother.

EUDOXIE: And you, Mister Artist, if I may give you a bit of advice?

MODI: Please, Madam.

EUDOXIE: Take care of my child.

MODI: I'll do my best, Madam, with the means I have.

EUDOXIE: No, you can do better.

MODI: I'll try… but after all, if your daughter was so happy at home, she wouldn't have come to live with this drunken wop.

EUDOXIE *(leaving the room)*: Oh!… How I detest you!

MODI *(going out and shouting)*: And I adore you!

Pause.

JEANNE: I don't like when you talk to her like that.
MODI: I can't speak any other way.
JEANNE: One day, you will need to improve your relationship.
MODI: Your mother and I have a very balanced relationship... she hates me as much as I hate her.
JEANNE: Promise me you'll make an effort.
MODI: I promise, my Jeanne. I'd know how to lie to her... after all, yesterday, I told Pablo I liked cubism.
JEANNE: But you love Pablo.
MODI: I love him and I hate him.
JEANNE: Will you ever love my mother?
MODI: One day, in ten years, when I'm old. I'll go to church on Sunday with her. I'll hold her hand and pray to her god.
JEANNE: I'm not asking for that much.
MODI: No chance, sweetheart: in ten years, I'll be dead.
JEANNE: Don't say that!
MODI: OK, enough about your mother. Worse things are happening than these quarrels. Sit down and listen! *(He grabs a chair, sits down, opens the newspaper.)* They've sworn to bring me down! Listen to this rubbish, this is what thousands of readers can see *(he reads)*: "To start with, Modigliani is not a painter"...
JEANNE: So what are you!?
MODI: Listen... that's only the beginning! *(Resuming)*: "He's a draughtsman who colours in his drawings".

JEANNE: You, a draughtsman!

MODI: Stop and listen! "Indeed, it is in his drawings that he is at his best". You can tell me the truth, Jeanne, do I have any talent? Even a small bit, really?

She says nothing.

MODI: You can tell me, I'm not a sensitive soul, you know.

She says nothing.

MODI *(reading again)*: "Modigliani exploits his sensibility…" *(Raising his head.)* Jeanne, I can be blamed for many things, but am I a sensitive person?... Compared to me, Kaiser Guillaume is a fickle boy… *(Reading again.)* "He exploits his… literary sensibility." And he calls me a literary person, on top of it. He confuses me with my mother, the holy woman, my mother, yes she's the scholar who translated all of D'Annunzio. But it's only Dante who I love. Dante is not literature, Dante is God who takes up his pen! *(Declaiming:)*

> *Quando Beatrice in sul sinistro fianco*
> *Vidi, vivolta e riguardar nel sole.*
> *Acquila si non li s'affisse unquanco.*

But this critic seems to know as much about literature as painting. *(He begins again.)* "And because he has a great sensitivity…" He insists, the monster!

But he should get information from the Queen Mother…

JEANNE: Continue.

MODI: "Modigliani is not likely to be too boring". And he thinks to compliment me! Jeanne, do you know someone more boring than me?… Chagall, eventually, yes, Chagall is more boring, but other than Chagall? Vlaminck, yes, in a different category, but then, I'm a close third. The third most boring man of Paris, and the greatest painter of the twentieth century…

JEANNE: Are you finished?

MODI: The worst is saved for the last! "When you see how Picasso and Derain have influenced him, you understand how impossible it is for Modigliani to ever be on an equal footing with them."… I'm less than Picasso! Less than Derain! And how can I defend myself? *(He takes a brush from the table and waves it in the air.)* Am I going to meet every reader and prove to him that I'm a painter? Do a portrait of every man who buys this trash? But I could, you know, I'm able!…

A silence.

MODI: Signed Clive Bell. He has the nerve to sign it! This guy should have died in Verdun. All Englishmen should have died in Verdun… The French are dead, the Germans decimated, but the English have survived everything. Dirty bastards!… He insults me and with me, he insults Italian painting, the entire Jewish people and the Livorno people. He insults Raphael, Caravaggio, Moses and David! And Brâncuși, my friend, my master!... A draughtsman!... When I dreamed of being a sculptor. When I paint it's to put some depth on the canvas! I paint because my lungs won't let me sculpt! I am a failure, Jeanne. I'm flat! *(He crumples the paper and throws it on the floor.)* Lower than Derain! Influenced by Picasso! I'd rather give up painting!

He flings the brush far away. Jeanne takes a cigarette from a packet on the floor, lights and smokes it. He gazes at her for a few seconds without saying anything.

MODI: I give up painting and you don't react?...

She quickly stubs the cigarette out on the floor.

MODI: Are you in cahoots with Clive Bell?

She smiles.

MODI: Are you smiling? They crush me and you smile. Women are even crueler than men! Worse than Clive Bell! You're lucky not to be English, being cruel like that!... You don't answer... are you taunting me? Are you thinking in silence? I speak, the English guy writes, and you, you think. At least he has a voice, this Bell, but you... you think in silence! You know I can't bear silence! I drink to drown the silence! You don't care! How could I have become infatuated with a woman like you who doesn't give a damn? At least with Clive Bell, he's not indifferent to me. He despises me, certainly, but he has feelings. You, you don't even despise me!

Pause.

JEANNE: With me, it's different.
MODI: Different?
JEANNE: You know it well.
MODI: I know nothing… you heard this Bell, barely good enough to draw.
JEANNE: I already told you.
MODI: Ah yes! That I'm mad?
JEANNE: Something else.
MODI: A brute? *(Pause.)* A boor?… A savage?… Ah I know, that I smell of alcohol!
JEANNE: A compliment.
MODI: Once, you told me you love my portraits of you.
JEANNE: Still something else.
MODI *(Pause)*: I don't see.
JEANNE: Go on!
MODI: Can't be about my friends. You hate my friends.
JEANNE: All of them.
MODI: Even Soutine?
JEANNE: Soutine I hate a bit less.
MODI: How can you hate Soutine? The wife of Zborowski I can understand, Madame of the Polish aristocracy, when she sees this good Jew just out of the ghetto,

blowing his nose on his shirt... But you, you should understand that Soutine is the greatest of geniuses.

JEANNE: I love you.

MODI: Sorry?

JEANNE: You heard me.

MODI: No, I have become deaf with age and alcohol.

JEANNE: I love your look, your power and your fear, I love the sparkle in your eye when you paint me, even if I know it's not me that you're looking at and not me that you're painting, that you're gazing into the abyss inside yourself. I am the woman of the moment. I love to be the woman of the moment though; your reason, the reflection of your soul... that's it. I love to be in your reflection.

MODI: The reflection?... but how do you come up with all this?... I have no reflection! I can't even look at myself in a mirror!... A reflection! I prefer it when you call me a drunk!... Would you strike a pose, please!

He bends, rearranges the brushes and the palettes on the table. He takes a brush.

MODI: I'm not going to let myself be butchered by an Englishman!

SCENE 3

Modi is painting Jeanne. We see him from the side. The easel is turned to the side too, the canvas invisible. A man, quite young, bearded, in a three-piece suit, a satchel under his armpit, enters the room. He's LÉOPOLD ZBOROWSKI.

ZBO: Hello Amedeo, Hello Jeannette.

> *Modi continues to paint, ignoring him.
> Jeanne doesn't move her head.*

ZBO: I have good news.

> *They don't react.*

ZBO: The best of the year 1917.

> *Silence.*

ZBO: I sold a painting to Berthe Weill!

> *No reaction.*

ZBO: The first painting sold for nine months.

> *No reaction.*

ZBO: Five hundred francs for the "Cello Player". Can you imagine, double what I got for the "Green Eyes". You will finally be able to pay your rent arrears. The owner has threatened me with jail if he doesn't get paid.

> *No reaction.*

ZBO: Five hundred francs, that's a good amount!

> MODI *puts his brush on the table, gets closer to* ZBO, *slowly but in a very threatening way.*

He comes up to ZBO*'s height, looks him in the eye, takes him by the collar, lifts him up a bit. Now coming face to face,* ZBO *terrorised.*

MODI: You interrupt me when I'm painting! And to talk about money! Do you remember that my great grandfather Emmanuel Modigliani was the banker for the Pope? Do you know, I told you a hundred times, that my grandfather Abraham Modigliani was Napoleon's adviser?! Napoleon! Do you know that you're sullying the art of a descendant of Baruch Spinoza?

ZBO *(lowered voice)*: Baruch Spinoza didn't have any descendants.

MODI: This Pole wants to teach me my own genealogy!... My great-aunt was called Régina Spinoza!

ZBO: Perhaps... but Baruch never had a child. So how can someone be a descendant in direct line?

MODI: And who's the line specialist in this world? Monet? Cézanne? Zborowski? No, the direct line is Modigliani! All my work is based on the line; that's what this Clive Bell faults in me. My line takes possession of space, my line has more than functional aesthetics, my line has an ethical role! And you claim I'm not a descendant of Spinoza? I descend along any line I like... It's not some Pole straight out of the shtetl who's going to tell me from where a Sephardi comes from!... I leave the best to Pablo. Mine is Baruch Spinoza! Anything to say?

ZBO *shakes his head.*

MODI: You want to dispossess me of my family legacy!?... As if it wasn't enough to steal my money and prevent me from painting... I told you a hundred times I forbid you to enter the room when I'm painting! You know I can't bear it. My attention is shattered, my brain gets scrambled, I become blind, blind and crazy! But you still do it! Tell me why?

ZBO: I didn't know...

MODI: Didn't you realise, ignoramus?

ZBO: I didn't know you were painting.

MODI: And what else would I be doing, huh? You're like Clive Bell, do you think I copy Derain's paintings?

ZBO *(his eyes fall on the crumpled newspaper)*: You could... have been reading the newspaper.

MODI: Will nothing stop this idiot? Do you know what is in the paper?

ZBO *(after some hesitation)*: If I don't come into the studio, how am I supposed to know what you're doing there?

MODI: And can't you think with your little cheap-art-dealer brain!? *(He taps his index finger on his skull while moving his ear closer.)* It rings hollow, listen, Jeannette, it rings hollow! How can I trust my paintings, my work, my life to someone who rings hollow? *(He lets go of ZBO.)*

ZBO: I'm sorry.

MODI: You can't help yourself! Some people ring hollow, that's all, don't apologise.

ZBO: For having entered, I mean.

MODI: I know you, you apologise, and then you'll do it again. You're like an ordinary mortal. You have no memory. That's the difference between us, who have too much memory: a mountain of memories, all the history of the world stuck in my head. That's why we paint, to let it out, this pile of shit other people just flush... OK, I'm not going to talk philosophy with a dealer who insults Spinoza... When I think you just cheated poor Berthe Weill. To give her a painting at triple its price! Now then, give me the five hundred francs, vile creature!

ZBO pulls his wallet from his pocket. He takes notes of one hundred francs out of it. He gives them, one by one, to MODI, carefully unfolding each.

ZBO: One hundred... two hundred... three hundred... and four hundred.

MODI keeps his hand stretched. ZBO puts his wallet in his satchel.

MODI *(tapping his index finger on ZBO's skull)*: Mr Zborowski, it seems to me the count is not accurate.
ZBO *(raising his head)*: Excuse me?
MODI: Look carefully, my dear Zbo, *(enumerating the notes)* one hundred francs... two hundred... three hundred... four hundred... this leaves a shortfall of?

ZBO stays silent.

MODI: Ah, maths is not the strong point of Mister Dealer... what's missing is...

ZBO: But and my... my commission!?
MODI: You mean that you're taking my money! So when I paint a woman with a hat, the hat is yours. This man is a hat thief, a highwayman! Do you know what we do with hat thieves? Jail!
ZBO: And... our agreement?
MODI: My hundred francs or I report you to the police! *(He grabs ZBO round the waist, shouts louder, as if to everyone at large.)* Police, Police, I caught the hat thief!
JEANNE: Stop, Dedo! Would you please let him go!
MODI: Never! He's an exploiter. And he sells paintings by Cézanne!

MODI tightens his grip.

MODI: Admit that you're selling paintings by Cézanne on the rue de Seine, and doing well out of it, nothing like five hundred francs a piece! Say it!
ZBO: There are some fans.
MODI: Mercenary, bad painting, scum! It's not that I dislike Cézanne. But you can't sell Cézanne AND Modigliani. You have to choose! Landscape OR portrait! You have to understand there is only man, God and man, and still nobody can represent God, it's written in the Bible, but Mr Zborowski has never read the Bible! He betrays his God and sells the Gods of your people for a hat. Renegade! Exploiter! *(He takes ZBO's wallet from his hands, seizes a hundred francs note and lets go of him.)* OK, go, and be happy

I let you go, thief!... Strike the pose again, Jeanne. We have to paint to feed these jackals and vultures.

He takes a gulp from the flask on the table, picks up a brush, gazes for a moment at JEANNE, *who has struck a pose again, turns around. He throws the notes he had in his hand at* ZBO.

MODI: And here, I don't want your charity!... All this has made me thirsty, I'm going down to La Rotonde. Bye, Jeanne. After all, perhaps you too only stay with me for the money!

He exits.

SCENE 4

After an embarrassing silence between JEANNE *and* ZBO.

JEANNE: Sometimes, I wonder why he stays with me.
ZBO: Why he stays with you?
JEANNE: Yes, why does he keep me with him? What do I give him? What does he feel for me?
ZBO: He was never very expressive... I mean, with feelings.
JEANNE: May I ask you a question?
ZBO: Anything you like.
JEANNE: Something about him... very personal. I will understand if you don't want to answer, if you wish to protect him.

ZBO: Amedeo hates people protecting him... Say it.
JEANNE: Well...
ZBO: Go on.
JEANNE *(firmly)*: He's cheating on me, isn't he!?
ZBO: Cheating on you? Him?
JEANNE: I'm sure he's cheating on me.
ZBO: What makes you think that?
JEANNE: Why would he be faithful? He's a ladies' man, isn't he?
ZBO: Men change, you know.
JEANNE: Yes, he changed. He spends his nights out. He's away for entire days... I'm sure he's seeing another woman.
ZBO: You know very well the name of his mistress.
JEANNE: Do you mean Beatrice?
ZBO: Beatrice has moved away.
JEANNE: Lunia, then. She's his lifelong companion.
ZBO: Nothing has ever happened with Lunia.
JEANNE: Do you know how many nudes of her he painted?
ZBO: Dozens.
JEANNE: And of me?

ZBO *stays silent.*

JEANNE: Not one. Are my curves less appealing than Lunia's?
ZBO: He respects you too much to show you nude. You are his only love, the only one... Along with...
JEANNE: Absinthe?
ZBO: Absinthe, rum, cocaine, opium and hashish, you're right... so many mistresses... *(A silence.)* And may I ask you a question?

JEANNE: Please.

ZBO: When he has his fits of rage, behaving like a brute, you… could you keep… your distance?

JEANNE: Where do you think I'd go?… Even if I could?

ZBO: Maybe to your parents' house?

JEANNE: Amedeo didn't tell you?

ZBO: Amedeo doesn't speak to me, he shouts at me, that's all.

JEANNE: I'm banned from my house. I'm in love with a drunkard whose escapades they read about in the newspapers!… And when they find out…

ZBO: When they find out what?

JEANNE: A gift from heaven, but for them a curse of God.

ZBO: Are you expecting…?

JEANNE: Will you keep it a secret?

ZBO: Will you keep the child?

EUDOXIE: How can you have any doubt?! I'll give Modigliani a son!… I'm sure it's a son. He kicks me with incredible force.

ZBO: When will you tell him?

JEANNE: I'm afraid of his reaction.

ZBO: He will be overjoyed.

JEANNE: Early on, yes, he will be proud. He will show off like a true Italian. He will parade boulevard Raspail, buy everyone a round, paint my round belly and make a cast of it, who knows? But later? He'll leave. He will never be a father.

ZBO: He will stay, you'll see.

JEANNE: May God hear you!

Muffled but violent explosions sound.

JEANNE: It's starting again.

ZBO: The Krauts are at the gates of Paris. But as long as the Big Bertha is booming, they won't be marching down the Champs-Élysées.

She strokes her belly.

JEANNE It's not good for the child. The earth is trembling, these explosions, this deprivation. And if the Germans come, you know what they do to women.

ZBO: Rumours…

JEANNE: They murder, they rape. Germans are barbarians. On the front, they drop gas in the trenches. My cousin came back blind… Oh, I'll end up with a bayonet in my stomach!

ZBO: The Italians hate Modigliani more than the Germans do.

JEANNE: Those are rumours.

ZBO: Never had one Italian buyer, and that's a fact. I think that's what offends Amedeo the most…

JEANNE: Everything hurts him. Dedo has been in pain since his birth.

ZBO: He can be hurtful too.

JEANNE: I dare you to say that in front of him!

ZBO: I'm sorry.

JEANNE: I'm teasing you. You are our benefactor, Léopold. Without you we would be sleeping in the Luxembourg Gardens, with all the rats… one of them almost bit me yesterday when I was walking with Dedo. I felt its mouth brushing against my leg. I cried out! Dedo grabbed the little beast and threw it across the park.

ZBO: You have to leave Paris.

JEANNE: We don't even have the fare for the Métro.

ZBO *(upon further reflection)*: You have to go to the South. I know people in Nice. For you, and for the baby, there's nothing better. And Amedeo will rediscover the light, and regain his health. Matisse is in the South, Renoir is in the South. And then, Nice is a bit like Italia. He talks so much about going back to Livorno.

JEANNE: Why not Livorno, then?

ZBO: Livorno, seeing his mother again, that's his greatest dream. Let him dream. That's what he's living for.

JEANNE: You think he's alive? He's more like a walking corpse! In the middle of the night, the whole building echoes with his coughs. He's got the disease, Léopold, and you know it. Tuberculosis has been eating away at him for the past ten years.

ZBO: We will send him to a sanatorium. He will be cured!

JEANNE: Yes, Léopold, and one day, all of Paris will come running to the Louvre to see "Girl with braids", and the portraits of Lunia.

ZBO: "Lying nude".

JEANNE: Yes, my good Léopold, that day will come, as will the day my father will hold my hand and walk me down the aisle.

ZBO: You see, you believe it too.

JEANNE: I'm very fond of you, Léopold, you are so good, and you also believe in the goodness of men.

ZBO: One day, I swear…

Enters MODIGLIANI, *with a firm step. He looks at* JEANNE, *then turns his gaze to* ZBO. *A moment of reflection.*

MODI *(with rage)*: Why didn't I think about this earlier?...
JEANNE: Think about what?
MODI *(keeping on)*: The dealer and the muse... I'm oblivious! I've left the wolf in sheep's clothing.
JEANNE: Does Léopold look like a wolf?
MODI: You call him Léopold, now? When I left you, it was Mr Zborowski. Things have moved fast...
JEANNE: You've been drinking.
MODI: I had nothing to drink. The owner of La Rotonde refused to serve me. He wants to be paid! For the poison he gives me! My wife sleeps with Zbo and the owner of La Rotonde demands payment! *(An explosion thunders.)* Go on, Krauts! Let the Big Bertha bang. Blow up Paris! It's Sodom, it's Gomorrah!
JEANNE: You have been drinking, I'm telling you!
MODI: No, I'm not drunk! And for once I can see clearly, and what I see... Two lovers in my studio... and when I'm not there, do you call him Léo? Dedo and Léo? Oh, a great joke that Cocteau will love! A brilliant painter without a penny meets a girl at La Rotonde, a poor lonely woman, dressed like a peasant; a little virgin, a saintly hypocrite, a Jeanne who listens to the voice of the artist and agrees to follow him home. He paints her, paints immense canvases and small portraits, he takes her under his roof, shares his bed, the one all the women dream of, and here we are... she sleeps with his patron!

ZBO: I won't let you say that!
MODI: I'm not taking any lessons in good manners from my wife's lover!

The gun thunders.

MODI: Go on, Krauts. Burn everything!... So, how long have you been playing this little game?
JEANNE: Don't answer him, he's out of his mind.
MODI: Oh, of course, I'm out of my mind. I catch you hand in hand, in my own studio!
JEANNE: Not only are you out of your mind, but you're also all sweaty. Come here so I can wipe your forehead.
MODI: You make me sweat. And now I'm seeing double.

He staggers. JEANNE *brings a chair closer.*

JEANNE: Sit down, my love, my impossible love.

ZBO *holds him by the shoulders.*

MODI *(pushing him back, standing up)*: Ah, don't touch me, you...!

MODI slowly collapses on the floor. ZBO holds him back so he doesn't hurt himself. He lays him on JEANNE's *lap, sitting on the floor.*

MODI *(in a quivering voice)*: I'm perfectly capable of crawling on the floor by myself!

JEANNE *wipes his forehead, caresses his face.*

JEANNE: My love, my sweet love.
MODI: I'm not the sweet love of anybody.

JEANNE: *(putting her hand on his forehead)*: You're burning hot. You have a fever. Léopold, call Doctor Alexandre.

ZBO leaves the room in a hurry.

MODI *(dozing off)*: I'm all right. It's just my head… and my eyes that can't focus. But the rest is fine. *(He holds out his trembling hands.)* Look. *(She takes his hands, kisses them.)*
JEANNE: My love. Don't worry, Doctor Alexandre will come and bring your fever down.
MODI: I don't need a…

He softly lays his head on JEANNE's lap, and dozes off.

ACT TWO

A cosy hotel room, with a balcony overlooking the seaside, the Promenade des Anglais. A view typical of Raoul Dufy's paintings. A bed. A small easel, a table. Canvases against a wall.

SCENE 1

JEANNE and her mother EUDOXIE.

EUDOXIE: You're going to be fine here. There is light, there is space. You will need space…

JEANNE stays silent.

EUDOXIE: Are you happy that I came down?

JEANNE nods yes.

EUDOXIE: You could say it, that you're happy.
JEANNE: I'm happy.
EUDOXIE: Because otherwise, I can go back, you know.
JEANNE: I know.
EUDOXIE: You make that decision.

JEANNE: Thank you.
EUDOXIE: I'm not expecting a thank you.

A silence.

EUDOXIE: Did you tell him in the end?
JEANNE: That the house brought bad luck?
EUDOXIE: Don't be nasty.
JEANNE: I'm echoing your words.
EUDOXIE: All of them?
JEANNE: I leave the worst to you. You don't get rid of bad luck that easily, you know.
EUDOXIE: If this gentleman Modigliani is still by your side, it's only because he still hasn't heard the news.
JEANNE: You're a pest, Mother.
EUDOXIE: A lying pest?
JEANNE: The plague, the cholera and the real truth.
EUDOXIE: And when do you intend to tell him? You realise that sooner or later it will be plain to see.
JEANNE: I'm waiting for a good time.
EUDOXIE: A good time with that man?
JEANNE: You can't possibly understand.
EUDOXIE: Yes, you're right, we have never been good at that, your father and I. You know, we have lived as best we could... Twenty years together, and two children...
JEANNE: A war hero and a social leper...
EUDOXIE: Two children we loved the best we could. But it's true, passion is not in our genes. I don't know where this burning inside you comes from... As for

us, we're deaf to great despair and intense joy. We haven't been invited to the feasts you talk about; we settle for leftovers. That's perhaps why we don't believe in heaven on earth.

JEANNE: So I'll go to hell?

EUDOXIE: You won't go anywhere. I'm here now.

JEANNE: To stop me from going to hell?

EUDOXIE: To be present, when he finds out and leaves you.

JEANNE: He won't leave me!

MODI enters.

MODI: Ah, you're here. If I knew, I'd have collected you at Nice station.

EUDOXIE: I didn't want to disturb you.

MODI: But you're still here.

EUDOXIE: I came to see my daughter.

MODI: How do you find her?

EUDOXIE: Sea air and heat look ravishing on her. You too, you've got a little bit of a tan.

MODI: And you, a little bit of awareness... In any case, I will be happy to take you back to the station.

EUDOXIE: You are too kind, my dear. Jeannette, I have to leave. Mr Zborowski has to show me to my hotel... Do you know where he is?

MODI: He's doing the rounds of luxury hotels, looking for buyers. That's his new whim. He says that the rich are not in Paris any more, they've left. They're all here, far from the front. He thinks they're in clusters, at the windows of the Negresco.

JEANNE: Mr Zborowski is taking care of us and that's how you treat him?

MODI: The defender of the weak, the oppressed and of art dealers has spoken.

EUDOXIE: I'll leave you. I'm going to wait for him at his hotel.

MODI: Don't forget, dear Madam, the day you go, I'm your man.

EUDOXIE: Don't worry, Amedeo, a man like you can't be forgotten... Goodbye, Jeanne.

JEANNE: Goodbye, Mother.

She leaves.

SCENE 2

JEANNE and MODI.

MODI *(with a false jubilation)*: You see, we're starting to get along.

JEANNE: One day, you won't be able to get enough of each other.

MODI: I'll do a portrait of her... I've never painted someone I detest.

JEANNE smiles.

MODI: Don't deny it! I made you laugh!

JEANNE: Saying your nasty things!
MODI: Something has changed in you.
JEANNE: It might be the heat or the sun.
MODI: No, it's something else.
JEANNE: I'm eating enough, here… I must have put on a bit of weight.
MODI *(he stares at her, a bit worried, takes two steps back)*: Can you stand up?
JEANNE: I'm quite comfortable here.
MODI: One thing troubles me.
JEANNE: Leave me be!
MODI: I would like to see something.
JEANNE: Very well, if you insist.

She gets up.

MODI: Straighten up.
JEANNE: Enough!

She sits down. MODI *bends his knees and crouching, walks around her. Jeanne is still and embarrassed.*

MODI: There's something wrong…
JEANNE: About me?

MODI continues to circle her, knees bent, examining her.

MODI: You have curves…
JEANNE: I always had curves, but you don't see them. You prefer Lunia.

MODI *(continuing to turn)*: ... Curves I didn't see before.
JEANNE: You know my curves by heart.
MODI *(continuing)*: New ones.
JEANNE: The Riviera works wonders.
MODI *(continuing)*: Your breasts...
JEANNE *(covering herself up)*: What about my breasts?
MODI *(continuing)*: Your belly...
JEANNE: I've put on weight, I told you.
MODI *(lifting his head)*: Your face...
JEANNE: Are you giving me an anatomy lesson?
MODI *(standing up)*: You are...!?
JEANNE: Jeanne, Jeanne Hébuterne, daughter of Achille Casimir and Eudoxie Anaïs Hébuterne...
MODI: Mother!... You are the mother of a little Modigliani! That's it! Tell me, you're pregnant?
JEANNE *(standing up and caressing her belly)*: I don't know where you got that idea.
MODI: You've made me... a father.
JEANNE: Normally we say: you've given me a child.
MODI: A father, me!
JEANNE: You!
MODI: And you didn't say anything!
JEANNE: You never let me talk.
MODI: You haven't shown me anything.
JEANNE: You don't look at me any more.
MODI: My mother will be overjoyed.
JEANNE: I'm delighted that your first thought is for her.
MODI: In Livorno, they'll hold a tremendous party! The Modigliani of the Modiglianis... and it's me who did it.

JEANNE: You didn't do it on your own...
MODI: I'm a father and you didn't say a word!
JEANNE: I thought of it silently.
MODI: Come into my arms, my wife!

JEANNE snuggles up against him.

JEANNE *(to herself)*: I just needed to be a mother...
MODI *(pushing her gently away)*: But... no... no! Lie down, you'll get tired.
JEANNE: It's only been a few weeks...
MODI: Lie down, I said!
JEANNE: You're not going to force me to lie in bed for six months?!
MODI: That's what you need.
JEANNE: You really are sick!
MODI: And a father. I'm a father. *(He steps back, holds his hand out to his imaginary double.)* Amedeo Modigliani, painter, father... No, better than that, Amedeo Modigliani, father.

JEANNE tries to sit up in the bed.

MODI: Please, don't move. You could...
JEANNE *(sitting up in bed, laughing)*: Lose him... Come, my sweet love of a father, lie on my knees. I'm safe, you know.
MODI: And him?
JEANNE: I'm strong enough for both of us.
MODI: Can you feel him moving?

JEANNE: Of course I can feel him.
MODI: Does he kick hard?
JEANNE: Very hard.
MODI: He'll be sturdier than me, taller than me.
JEANNE: Taller won't be difficult.
MODI: You can make fun of me. I'm now the strongest man in the world.
JEANNE: Who ever doubted it?
MODI *(lifting his head)*: Would you make that gesture again that women do, caress your belly? A lullaby, with your hands…
JEANNE *(caressing her belly)*: Like this?
MODI: I could watch you for hours.
JEANNE *(continuing her movement)*: What should we name him?
MODI: Isaac, like my grandfather. It's a tradition at home.
JEANNE: Your grandfather was crazy, right?
MODI: Everyone is a bit crazy in my family… another tradition.
JEANNE: Isaac is fine with me, even if your grandfather was insane.
MODI: If it's a girl, we'll have the same problem.
JEANNE: It won't be a girl.
MODI *(counting on his fingers)*: My aunt Laura… interned in Milan… my aunt Gabriella… committed suicide in Rome… Margherita, my own sister, has a persecution complex… feeling persecuted is terribly common among Jewish people.
JEANNE: In a world where anti-Semitism is very common.
MODI: Ancient history… The ghetto, the Dreyfus case and

the pogroms! It's 1917. It's time for a global revolution. The Russians are leading the way. Next it will be the Italians. Then the Germans will assassinate the Kaiser. No more nation, no more war! Isaac will live in a world where Jews will be forgotten.

JEANNE *(pensive)*: Isaac is very beautiful, very noble. He won't be crazy.

MODI: Anyway, with us, it's either the asylum or tuberculosis. My grandmother Olympia spat blood, my uncle Amedeo had a massive haemoptysis.

JEANNE: If I get to choose for my son, I would prefer madness.

MODI: My grandfather taught me everything.

JEANNE: He taught you suspiciousness.

MODI: You find me suspicious!?

JEANNE: No, no… suspicious is not the word.

MODI: What's the word, then?

JEANNE: … Moody?

MODI: Me, moody!? No, Soutine is moody. Pablo is moody. Me, I'm just sceptical. That's me, I'm sceptical.

JEANNE: We can say you are a great sceptic.

MODI: You can't be a half-sceptic.

JEANNE: And you're not. You are a wholly uncompromising person.

MODI: Being wholly uncompromising is a flaw?

JEANNE: Not in your case.

MODI: Because if you prefer, I can be… what is the opposite of whole?

JEANNE: Empty.

MODI: I can be empty, if you prefer.

JEANNE: No, no, I like you more as a whole person. *(She brings her face and her lips close to* MODI's.*)* All mine.
MODI: Here in any case. Even if I wanted to... who could I belong to?
JEANNE: To the fishmonger of rue Massena.
MODI: The baker of rue Gambetta.

She bursts out laughing. She caresses her belly. He looks at her belly.

MODI: He will be...
JEANNE: A scientist. A great one. An Italian Einstein.
MODI: A scientist!?
JEANNE: We will be fed up with paintings. You will be more famous than Matisse and Pablo. And I will have given up painting my daubs.
MODI: You're not painting daubs. Your characters are alive, your landscapes speak. Your paintings face the truth. Even if you're a witch.
JEANNE: A witch?
MODI: You've put a spell on me. I'm not looking at women any more. I'm not drinking any more. I've become a good little boy. Despite a fragile exterior, you're stronger than my mother, stronger than a Jewish Italian mama!... A witch, I tell you. And one who cures people as well. I barely spit blood any more.
JEANNE: And you accept being a father...
MODI: You think this will last?
JEANNE: Forever.
MODI *(more sombre, after a pause)*: You know well that

one day, the demons will come back. On that day, you'll take our son for a walk on the Promenade des Anglais. That day, I'll be thirsty... even though you're a witch, you won't be able to do a thing about it!

JEANNE: I will repel your demons, and Bacchus, and the god of opium. Look: *(she lays her hand on her belly)* I'm the goddess of fertility. And demons can't do anything against such divinity.

MODI: They're going to swoop down on me, dangling barrels of red wine and wagon-loads of mistresses.

JEANNE: I'll be stronger than your demons. Do you realise the immensity of my love?... Come, I'll show you.

She stands up, takes MODI *by the hand and leads him to the window.*

JEANNE: Bigger than infinity. *(A short moment at the window.)*

MODI: Come in, sun isn't good for the baby... Lie down...

JEANNE lies down, a smile on her face.

MODI: Wouldn't you like to make that gesture with your belly...

She caresses her belly. He stares at her.

MODI: Stay like that, so I can paint you.

SCENE 3

Someone knocks on the door.

MODI: It's open!

ZBO enters.

MODI: Ah, here's the other one who has the nerve to come in!
ZBO: You told me...
MODI: I said: it's open, I didn't say to come in.
ZBO: I thought...
MODI: You thought wrong, and I didn't know it was you. Why don't you announce when it's you?
ZBO: I knocked.
MODI: And how do I know it's you knocking?
JEANNE *(smiling)*: Are you going to leave him alone?
ZBO: I was just coming to tell you some good news.
JEANNE: The war is over?
ZBO: No, the war isn't over, even if the Germans are retreating.
MODI: I know... Picasso is dead!
JEANNE: I don't like it when you're so cynical.
MODI: I'm not cynical, I'm enquiring about my fellow painter's health. I'm paying attention, but you don't know anything about attention. You don't care. All you care about is this damned war...
ZBO: Of course, you, you are not interested in war.
MODI: What are you suggesting!?

ZBO: I never suggested anything.

JEANNE: Don't get excited, Dedo! Mr Zborowski is not the type of man to insinuate things.

MODI: Oh yes he is, he's just that type of man! Look at his false face. I know it well, I painted a portrait of it. I know what he's suggesting. By the way, you understood what he meant too!

ZBO: I wasn't trying to suggest anything.

MODI: You talk without meaning to say anything! A liar and a coward, as well as being a thief! You know I broke a policeman's jaw for less than that.

ZBO: I know that, I came to collect you at the police station. And I paid the fine, too.

MODI: Always the money! Zbo, how you shame me! So tell me, even Jeanne got it. You're insinuating that I didn't take part in this war, aren't you?

ZBO: Absolutely not!

MODI: I'm not interested in news from the front because I didn't have the courage to go to the front, is that it?

JEANNE: Stop it, Dedo.

MODI: I sat on my backside behind my easels. You're right to call me a coward.

ZBO: I never said that!

MODI: You thought it so loudly that even the fishmonger on rue Gambetta heard you. And it's true, they all enlisted, are all wallowing in the mud of the trenches while I get a tan in front of the Westminster Hotel.

ZBO: Pablo didn't go either.

MODI: Cowardly like Picasso, as if that's going to console me! And Guillaume, did he just sit and watch the

Seine on Pont Mirabeau? No, he went and took a bullet in his head, rightly so. He behaved like a man, Guillaume. Don't try to catch the seagulls on the Bay of Angels!

ZBO: Guillaume is at his worst, you know, Spanish flu.

MODI: Apollinaire has left us. Braque got a bullet in the head. Kisling got a bayonet in his chest. Cendrars lost an arm. Zadkine was gassed at the front, and even the Krauts... Macke, wounded and Franz Marc killed in Verdun. And I stay quietly at home!

JEANNE: You volunteered, it's not your fault if...

MODI: And why did they reject me? I can't be killed like the others. I'm somehow worse than Franz Marc?

JEANNE: You know perfectly well why.

MODI: My lungs! They send everybody to die, but they refuse to sign up the sick, even if the job is already half done... me, the king wop, the prince of Montparnasse, my only war-wound is getting sunburnt on the seafront!

A silence.

JEANNE: Dear Zborowski, tell us your good news and we'll tell you ours as well!

MODI: No, he won't say anything, he'd rather just call me a deserter!

ZBO: So OK... but be aware, don't jump for joy... nothing is signed yet... But well, we're moving forward. *(Proudly.)* We have been selected for the International Exhibition in London!

MODI: Who, us?

ZBO: I mean… your paintings.

MODI: And my paintings are "us"!?

JEANNE: Let him finish, would you?!

ZBO: I received a telegram from the Commissioner of the fair, Osbert Sitwell. It will take place next summer.

MODI *(next lines, as an aside)*: In a year? Posthumously?

ZBO: … Sitwell is organising an exhibition with the main painters of the Paris School.

MODI: I don't belong to any school.

ZBO: … In the Mansard Gallery.

MODI: And I'm not Parisian.

ZBO: … There will be Matisse, Picasso…

MODI: Never heard of them.

ZBO: … Amedeo will be the star of the exhibition. Sitwell would like to take more than a dozen of his works compared to only three of Picasso's…

MODI: The English are good people, after all.

ZBO: … Your paintings will be in pride of place.

MODI: British taste… excellent.

ZBO: … For London's richest buyers.

MODI: And visionary…

ZBO: … This exhibition, is going to change everything.

MODI: Why do you all try to change me?

JEANNE: Exhibited at last… and in London. You should be happy, Dedo!

MODI: Happy to be exhibited? Zbo, can you tell Jeanne about the success of my previous exhibition?

ZBO: Which one?

MODI: How many times have I exhibited, you cheap art dealer?

ZBO *(lowered voice)*: Once.

MODI: Tell her, she'll understand why I'm not jumping for joy at your news!

ZBO: But that was... different.

MODI: No, different is not the right word. It was catastrophic, dramatic, comic, stupid, hilarious, appalling. Tell her!

ZBO: I don't know how to tell a story I'm not very good at telling.

JEANNE: Tell it, you know it.

MODI: OK, by popular demand... *(He stands up, takes a sort of bow, and with his voice declaiming.)* The story of the first and no doubt last exhibition by Amedeo Modigliani, wop painter, prince of Montparnasse and of my ass, outstanding portrait painter, descendant of Baruch Spinoza and of Isaac the screwed, of no fixed address but with a good address book, friend of great men and of women of easy virtue, a connoisseur of primitive art, and a primitive himself... therefore, in December of the Great German War, which did as much for humanity as the little Spanish flu, Mr Zborowski, artists' thief is his current profession, successfully managed to exhibit Sir Modigliani and only him, and without the others who eclipse him on the terraces of Montmartre. Duly noted. The exhibition took place courtesy of the good Berthe Weill, another Big Bertha, the canon of French art, who discovered Van Gogh, Van Dongen as well as the Fauvists, but nobody's perfect... Madame Weill had agreed to take on the great Modi, with his five-foot-six figure, his bad breath, his repulsive manners and admirable paintings. Inside the gallery, it should have been a bacchanalia of the senses, recognition and ecstasy, at 50 rue Taitbout, on the ground floor to the right, you can't miss it... the good Berthe had selected, from the illustrious but unknown genius, not one, not two, but eighteen paintings, and Mr Zborowski had promised that by selling half of them, we would be as rich as Croesus. For us, beautiful neighbourhoods, carriages and furs, Marquesas Islands. For us, money, glory, and Paris on its knees! The faith of Zbo!

ZBO: This is too much!

MODI: It's nothing!... and this is what happened... Zbo, this imperial strategist, this Carpathian genius! This idiotzwki! This smooth talker thought a good idea to draw crowds would be to put some big sumptuous nudes on display in the window, some magnificent Modis, women offered openly and publicly to the onlookers... and the result was beyond his highest hopes! They all rushed to Gallery Weill, all of Paris together, the powerful, critics, ministers and bankers, Marcel Sembat, Kahnweiler and Raynal, André Simon. Once inside the room, all the wise collectors swooned over the paintings, admired the deep lines in space. How delighted they were, these jaded people, these gossips, they were going to take it all, and the feast would be ours... so said the dealer...

ZBO: I'm leaving!

MODI: Stay, or I'll make you eat my brushes!... And soon, do you know, my Jeanne, mother of all my children, motherland of my love?... Seeing the place stuffed with these rich idlers, war profiteers, with full bellies and fat wallets, a few passers-by gathered, poor wretches without any taste but with an appetite... and, oh, what did they see? In the window and then inside, these dumbfounded onlookers who had never seen anything like it before? Naked women, fully naked, embodying sensual pleasures, things they'd never seen in their wildest dreams, naked women lying along rue Taitbout. And soon, there was a crowd, shouting "oh", "ah", "yuck"; or calling out in outrage... *(Softer.)*

The riot drew the attention of a particularly glorious commissioner, Rousselot was his name, a cop who hated the ladies. The pig-guardian of moral order and peace of mind, who immediately summoned the good Bertha. Here's what they said: *(High voice.)* – What have I done wrong? *(Low voice.)* – Madam Weill, don't play the innocent! – I really don't see how you haven't realised. – Your window! – Never seen any nude paintings? – I order you to remove them! – Have they done something wrong? – Nudes! But you must be blind!? – These naked women... have hair! So all the posh gentlemen had to take down all the exhibited nudes themselves, watched by the cops and the morally-damaged people outside. And the exhibition, my first, my great one which was supposed to ensure forever the fame and fortune of the Modigligenius, supposed to run for a month, was immediately shut down after the first day! And all because the women had hair...! That's it, my dear, now you know about the only time ever that Modigliani had a solo exhibition... *(Yelling at* ZBO.*)* And you still dare to appear before me?

JEANNE *(towards* ZBO*)*: It's not your fault, dear Léopold, it was circumstance.

MODI: Circumstance, my ass!

ZBO: Is that the end of the story?

MODI: Not yet! You understand why, my sweet, I'm not jumping for joy upon getting the news of being exhibited in London. Speaking from experience, whatever remains from Victorian England will spit and slash my paintings... Zbo, if you take any of my nudes, you'll be dog meat!

JEANNE *(softly)*: And our good news about us?

MODI: Jeanne, I'll let you make the announcement. I'm going out. I've talked too much and it's made me thirsty.

SCENE 4

In the hotel room, MODI *and* EUDOXIE, *alone. They are having lunch at a table. Long silence. They eat without looking at each other.* MODI *chews noisily. He serves himself with his fingers. He wipes his nose with his napkin.* EUDOXIE *very ladylike, eyes on her plate.*

EUDOXIE *(finally raising her head on* MODI*)*: You're not so unpleasant really.
MODI: And you, I'm sure people would have found you charming.
EUDOXIE: You know how to talk to women.
MODI: You have... *(He leans forward and stares at her.)* You have... something of Jeanne.
EUDOXIE: You mean the opposite.
MODI *(sits back in his chair)*: The opposite is true too, you lack the immense beauty of Jeanne.

Silence. They eat.

EUDOXIE: Do you think my daughter deliberately left us alone together?
MODI: You know her better than me.
EUDOXIE: Since you met, she's unrecognisable.
MODI: And of course, that's because of me.
EUDOXIE: Whose fault is it, then?
MODI: What you don't know is that Jeanne is stronger than me. She's the one who transforms me. Look. *(He raises his hands above his plate.)*
EUDOXIE: I don't see anything.
MODI: She doesn't see anything!... But it's obvious!

He keeps his hands up.

EUDOXIE: You have beautiful hands, strong and thin hands, the hands of an artist.
MODI: This I know! But what else is it about these hands?...

(as if to himself.) This woman is blind!... OK, I'll tell you, they're not shaking!

EUDOXIE: Indeed.

MODI: Your daughter works wonders. She transforms wine into water... Jeanne is a witch.

EUDOXIE: Let's say a healer.

MODI: I'm not sure she can cure my sickness.

EUDOXIE: In any case, you don't shake any more and you've stopped drinking.

MODI: I drank because I was shaking... I was shaking from the inside. But you can't understand.

EUDOXIE: Of course, simple people like me have no inner life.

MODI: People think they have one but they're confused. Someone with an inner life is someone who's being devoured inside, a stranger inside, an enemy.

EUDOXIE *(ironic)*: The enemy from within?

MODI: Make fun if you like! You don't suffer anybody, you!

EUDOXIE: But of course! While you endure all the misery of the world. Even mine. Everything is yours. Other people are simpletons, happy simpletons. Amedeo, let me tell you something: you think you know everything. You're nothing, but an... ill-mannered person... Oh, how I hope Jeanne's baby won't take after you... Well, will you...

MODI: Will I what?

EUDOXIE: Your child...

MODI: My son!

EUDOXIE: Your... son... do you intend to register him?

MODI: Even if it's a girl!... You doubt I would?

EUDOXIE: You don't usually admit to anything.

MODI: I told you, your daughter has changed me...

EUDOXIE: You seem happy.

MODI: I am, morning and night, dear Madam... From the beginning of the week, to midnight on Sunday... On Monday, I start by... Do you want to know?

EUDOXIE: I would like to.

MODI: On Monday at 2:00 sharp, I begin to stroll on the Promenade des Anglais. I go from the Negresco up to the port. And once I get to the port, do you know what I do?... I come back! That is my blissful Monday. Do you want to know about Tuesday?

EUDOXIE: Please.

MODI: On Tuesday, I stroll on the Promenade des Anglais. Do you know where I leave from?

EUDOXIE: From the Negresco?

MODI: Perceptive... I walk up to the port. Then, I come back. That's my blissful Tuesday.

EUDOXIE: Where are you going with all this?

MODI: To Wednesday.

EUDOXIE: Be serious!

MODI: Do I look like I'm laughing?... Before, oh, yes! Before, in my other life, when I was alive, without a wife or a child, I went to the Closerie des Lilas or La Rotonde and passed out laughing. All of Montmartre was in stitches when I walked by. Today... I make even a dead fish cry.

EUDOXIE: Why don't you go and see people? The whole world is in Nice.

MODI: Ah, but I've seen a lot of people, and even the king of the world.

EUDOXIE: Did you see Matisse?
MODI: Matisse wasn't there. I went to see Renoir.
EUDOXIE: You've seen Renoir!?
MODI: As plain I see you now.
EUDOXIE: Tell me!
MODI: No.
EUDOXIE: Why not?
MODI: Because I have been mocked enough.
EUDOXIE: Am I someone who likes to mock?
MODI: You're the kind of woman who sniggers. You're ironic and rude.
EUDOXIE: Rude?
MODI: Not once, but twice.
EUDOXIE: If it's like that, don't say anything.
MODI: You don't want to know?
EUDOXIE: Not at all.
MODI: My life doesn't interest you?
EUDOXIE: Not that much.
MODI: Modigliani and Renoir in the same room at the same time, it doesn't pique your curiosity?
EUDOXIE: Two painters are no better than anyone else.
MODI: The meeting of two giants, one in the twilight years of his grandiose life, the other at the dawn of immense glory, it leaves you unimpressed!?
EUDOXIE: You're bound to embellish things.
MODI: Professional courtesy.
EUDOXIE: To tell you the truth, with a bit of psychology, I can imagine the scene.
MODI: You, a psychologist!? I thought you were a housewife.

EUDOXIE *(without noting)*: So, first of all... I'm sure things ended badly.

MODI: Here we go!

EUDOXIE: You're the kind to make situations even worse.

MODI: Before perhaps... not any more.

EUDOXIE: Did the meeting end well?

MODI: Through no fault of my own.

EUDOXIE: You're never guilty of anything... All this misfortune falling on you. It's because you're a stranger, a Jew, a painter or whatever. You never feel guilty about anything.

MODI: Go on.

EUDOXIE: Well I can see you arriving in Cagnes-sur-Mer and going into Renoir's house, your head bowed. You are already pissed the moment you walk through the door. In fact, you're not comfortable being around the ageing genius. You are afraid.

MODI: Me, afraid?!

EUDOXIE: You are thinking, is that the way painters end their lives? In a wheelchair, impotent. Is it worth the pain, so much effort and tears, to end up like that?

MODI: Go on, you interest me.

EUDOXIE: You are introduced to the old man. You make him smile. He sees himself at the same age; arrogant, pretentious.

MODI: Stop it, I've heard too much. I'm going to tell you the real truth.

EUDOXIE: Unnecessary, I know it. Jeanne told me everything.

MODI: Phew, for a second I thought you were a psychic. You're not troubled about pulling my leg?

EUDOXIE: It makes a change from the Promenade des Anglais.

MODI: OK, it's fair game, I don't blame you, but tell me what Jeanne said.

EUDOXIE: You're going to blame her.

MODI: I always need someone to detest. And this morning, I like you. Tell me! So I can set the record straight.

EUDOXIE: First of all, YOU were dying to see Renoir.

MODI: Not wrong.

EUDOXIE: You ordered this Mr Ostering to lead you to Cagnes-sur-Mer.

MODI: What's wrong with that?

EUDOXIE: Renoir was waiting for you, wallowing in his chair, his hat on his head, his face wrapped in a mosquito net.

MODI: He was afraid I'd bite him.

EUDOXIE: You examined the paintings hanging on the wall for a long time.

MODI: Exhibiting your own paintings at home! And I'm the arrogant one!?

EUDOXIE: Renoir asked you: "So, you're a painter yourself, young man?"

MODI: Did I ask him if he was a carpenter himself?

EUDOXIE: Then, he gave you some advice.

MODI: I didn't ask for anything.

EUDOXIE: He said: "Paint with joy, with the same joy you have in loving a woman."

MODI: How would he have dealt with Cocteau?

EUDOXIE: And since you were silent, Renoir did the talking for you, and he said: "Caress your canvas for a long time. I touch the buttocks for days before finishing a painting."

MODI I don't like buttocks myself.

EUDOXIE: It's exactly what you dared to say to Renoir before leaving the villa! You said: "I don't like buttocks myself!" and then slammed the door!

MODI: Absolutely!

EUDOXIE: You were lucky to be invited to see Renoir, who never sees anybody, and who's going to die soon. You could have learned about him and his work; received his opinion, some advice, anything. Built a relationship, a friendship, the old man and the young man… and the only thing you managed to say, the only words that came out of your mouth were: "I don't like buttocks myself!"

MODI: He shouldn't have provoked me. Besides, I'm not going to lie, it's true that I don't like buttocks. Have you ever seen any buttocks in my paintings?

EUDOXIE: I haven't seen all your nudes.

MODI: Of course you haven't: none have sold. The canvases are at Zbo's, piled up, one on top of the other, it's so embarrassing. Ask for my nudes, look at them face to face, you'll see. I paint breasts, I paint the pubis, I even paint pubic hair, but you would find only two pairs of buttocks, two naked women lying on their back. And still, one is only half-turned, so it's only one buttock actually, I add two of them; that makes three, or one-and-a-half pairs if you prefer… Versus thirty or forty pairs of breasts, the count is accurate… I have my reasons, you know, the first is a question of pride, I don't like buttocks being shown to me. The second is a question of art, the buttock eats the face, it takes the limelight from it, it steals the thunder, and it takes up all the space. The third… there's no third, but two is ample… So, this Mr Renoir, this senile old man with a mosquito net, is not going to lecture me. I don't take lessons about buttocks from anybody!

EUDOXIE: You are beyond redemption!
MODI: But I don't want to be redeemed!
EUDOXIE: Nobody's trying to redeem you.
MODI: So, we agree. In the end, buttocks have reconciled our differences.

Embarrassed silence from EUDOXIE.

EUDOXIE: I think I'm going to leave.
MODI: The pleasure is all mine.
EUDOXIE: Give my regards to my daughter.
MODI: And your farewells too.

She leaves the room. He wipes his mouth with his napkin, a bit messily. He eats, stops.

MODI: It's not Renoir who's going to teach me painting!

ACT THREE

SCENE 1

In the darkness of the hotel room. We see MODI *lying down on the bed.* JEANNE *enters. She walks over to the window.*

JEANNE: Why are you in the dark?
MODI *(turning)*: I can't bear the light.

She pulls back the curtains a little.

JEANNE: It's a beautiful day.

He puts a pillow over his head.

MODI: I'm telling you, I don't like the light here.
JEANNE: The light from the South!?
MODI: Yes, it's too vivid, it blinds me.

She pulls back the curtains further, to the middle.

JEANNE: People from all over the world are coming here for it. Americans, Russians, King George the Fifth…

MODI: Well, I'm not the Queen of England! *(More quietly.)* Here, the light is too pure. It dazzles me. It prevents me from seeing clearly... If only it was just the light. But there's all this blue.

JEANNE: This blue?

MODI: You look up, the blue of the sky, you look down, the Big Blue. How am I supposed to paint surrounded by all this blue?... In Paris, the sky is nowhere to be found, or it melts into the grey... it doesn't disturb you. I can concentrate on my faces.

JEANNE: Matisse and Picasso came here for the blue and the light.

MODI: Oh please, don't compare me with them! I detest comparisons.

JEANNE: I didn't mean to offend you.

MODI: Too late.

JEANNE: You would like... to go back. I will follow you, you know, I'll go back with you.

MODI: And you'll give birth on the train? And our son will die of hunger, of cold, if he's not buried by the bombs... No, no, I can't move, I'm done for, chained, a prisoner, a husband. That's the exact term; I'm a husband... *(Lowered voic*e.) Jeanne's husband.

JEANNE: I can stay on my own, you know... my mother's here. You can leave. I don't want to force you to do anything.

MODI: Right, and leave my son in the arms of your... this woman who detests me? No, no, give birth and at least we'll be able to leave from here to go to Livorno. Once we're in Livorno, everything will be better. My mother will raise the child. She will make a real Modigliani out of him; someone brave and well read, a rebel and an artist. And there, I'll build a house, I'll erect a marble edifice, cut from stone, not like Rodin with his casts... I'll sculpt the walls and the insides of the walls; it will be the most beautiful house in Livorno.

JEANNE: But didn't you leave Livorno?

MODI: It was a mistake. One should never leave Livorno.

JEANNE: You left to become somebody.

MODI: Somebody? A wreck, a parasite...

JEANNE: An amazing painter...

MODI: And you've seen the last works of this unknown genius, the Raphael of the Bay of Angels, the da Vinci of the Promenade des Anglais... *(He gets up, walks towards the end of the room, where five or six paintings are arranged one against the other. He takes up one of them, one of the only four landscapes ever painted by Modigliani in the South, called "Trees and house". He shows her the painting.)* What do you see?

JEANNE: A painting... very beautiful.

MODI: That's irrelevant!

JEANNE: A landscape.

MODI: You're not surprised?

JEANNE: It's a beautiful landscape.

MODI: Have you seen me painting a landscape before?

JEANNE: I don't think so.

MODI: Focus, Jeanne. Since we met, have you seen one painting of mine which is a landscape?

JEANNE: ... Not that I can remember.

MODI: You saw my old paintings at Zbo's. As far as you can recall, did you come across a single landscape?

JEANNE: It's likely I didn't.

MODI: It's likely you didn't! Never in all my life, I have never painted landscapes! I hate landscapes! I have only painted men, women, children, old people, whores, soldiers... Only the human interests me. I can paint expressions. Have you ever seen a landscape with an expression? Has a tree ever talked to you? To me, never! Trees don't express themselves in front of me. They speak poorly. They must understand that I don't like them. They stay silent and dry, they take revenge... And then, after three months here, I start to paint them. It's as if the Prince of Wales was having a shit in the middle of the Promenade des Anglais!

JEANNE: You have painted four landscapes, it's not the end of the world!

MODI: I think you don't get it... What do you see in this painting?

JEANNE: A house...

MODI: And nothing upsets you about this house?

JEANNE: It's a beautiful house, simple but beautiful.

MODI: Do you notice anything!?... It doesn't have a door, a window – this house! For Christ's sake, you're as blind as your mother!... And look here, what's that?

JEANNE: A window, a long window...

MODI: An arrow-loop! I didn't know it myself when I was painting, but it's so obvious... What else is on this canvas!?

JEANNE: ... A tree.

MODI: What is the tree like?

JEANNE: You could say it's not blooming... It's winter...

MODI: Dry! Dead! A dead tree... And these colours, grey... a dead tree, a prison cell, a desert landscape! Here is the last Modigliani! Even Zbo won't recognise his painter. You have made me unrecognisable!... Even your mother is getting to like me, the saintly woman who saw me as the prince of perverts, a sane woman then, Eudoxie Hébuterne now praises me.

JEANNE: She merely says you have found your lust for life again.

MODI: But I hate the lust for life! I drink to get that taste out of my mouth. *(He points to the painting.)* Look what it does to me, this lust for life: a dead landscape!

JEANNE *(taking his hand and laying it on her belly)*: I thought I was doing the right thing...

MODI: You're all the same in your family, to do good on earth... Your father with his prayers and devotion, and your saintly mother! You're beating me down with your kindness... But you, I thought you were different. That's why I chose you. Your despair jumped out at me when I saw you at La Rotonde... I thought I'd found a true soulmate... with your look so sad... the Madonna with the Infant Jesus!... But no, you're just like the others, you women, you're made for life, to give life...

JEANNE: I don't want you to see me like other women...

MODI *(he goes to draw the curtains back entirely)*: I can't see anything any more with this light.

JEANNE: Come, lie down beside me. *(She lies down on the bed.)* Promise me you won't treat me like you treat other women?

She caresses her belly a long time. He stands up gazing at her for a moment. He picks up a quilt, lies down on the floor near the bed, puts his head under the pillow, and stays like that.

SCENE 2

A cradle in the middle of the room lit by a bright light outside. The bawling of a newborn child. And in the distance, an atmosphere of celebration, music, trumpet, cheers. On the small table, a bottle of wine and a full glass. JEANNE *rushes and takes the baby in her arms. She cradles the baby.*

JEANNE: My baby, don't cry, my brightness, my delight. Why are you so sad, my joy, my other love? *(She goes to the window.)* There is no reason, my Jeanne. Look… behind the window… the sky is a cake full of immense sweetness. *(She comes back.)* My child, my life, press your small face against my breast and listen to my heart, it beats only for you, your big velvet eyes, and your small bare feet. *(She stops cradling, goes to the table, seizes the glass and drinks half of it. More crying.)* Your face is that of an angel full of mysteries. My girl, keep your beautiful eyes open, you are the new world full of ancient treasures… My Jeanne, my other me, is your mother crying? *(She seizes the glass again, finishes it.)* There is no reason to be sad. I will dry your tears. *(She goes to the window again.)* Look, outside, jubilant crowds… Peace has come the month you were born. War is over, my Jeanne, my love, it's the end of wars!… Tomorrow, we will go dancing in the middle of a crowd, we will celebrate the victory, the very last one… *(She fills her glass and drinks half of it. She sits.)* But today, I feel tired… Oh, my baby, my joy, tell me, is it your fault that Dedo has left? Is it you who made him run away, my sweet, my soul? *(She finishes her drink.)* Is there a devil hidden in you? My man disappeared when you had barely appeared. *(She holds the baby with both hands, stares at her. The baby stops her cries.)* But no, what do I say?! Your eyes speak for you. Anyone would be crazy to leave such a beauty! I'm making you feel guilty, you, innocence itself… Sorry, my Jeanne. Your mother is a bad woman. It's a shame to accuse a little girl like that.

EUDOXIE enters the room, a basket in her hand, she puts it down.

EUDOXIE: Shameful! As you say. How can you talk like that to your child? You think she doesn't understand?!… This girl doesn't have a father and her mother curses her!?… *(She sees the wine bottle.)* And now, you're drinking?!… The vandal leaves you, abandons the child and leaves you his bad habits?

The child has stopped crying, JEANNE *lays her in the cradle.*

JEANNE: He never left me, Mother. He had to go back.
EUDOXIE: Of course.
JEANNE: Do you want to read his letters?
EUDOXIE: What a smooth talker! So, look me in the eyes and tell me, Jeanne, you're drinking wine, now?
JEANNE: I was thirsty.
EUDOXIE: That man…! He's the devil himself!
JEANNE: You're talking about my…
EUDOXIE: About what? Your husband? Did I miss something like a ceremony?
JEANNE *(lowering her eyes)*: You didn't miss anything… he's the father of my child, the man you call a devil!
EUDOXIE: I've certainly missed something! I am the one who wrote on the birth certificate. I had to put down something, a trifle, remember… Yes, it comes back to me: "Father unknown"… But perhaps I'm wrong? Perhaps now this man did recognise his daughter?
JEANNE *(more lowered voice)*: You know very well that he didn't… Why are you tormenting me?
EUDOXIE: He's tormenting you. He distresses your daughter, he tortures your mother. This man is a torturer… Oh, I can still hear him, "I'll register my son… even if it's a girl!"
JEANNE: He ran out of time.
EUDOXIE: Of course! Sir is so busy! Cafes are closing so late! You think I didn't see he went back to drinking. Obviously this time, he's got somebody with him.

JEANNE: I would be in Paris, if I was with him.

EUDOXIE: But yes, why didn't I think of that? Go back to Paris. Your daughter is big now, she can take care of herself... Is it true what they say... you have begun to search for a nanny? You are preparing your escape...

JEANNE *(hesitant)*: I want to join him, Mother...

EUDOXIE: Face it, my daughter: he's gone to Paris to get away from you, from you and this child he never wanted.

JEANNE: You don't know what you're talking about. He went to get some money, for us three to be able to live together, and one day... *(Proudly straightening up.)* One day, we'll go and live in Italy in a marble palace...

EUDOXIE: Dreams, my girl, dreams...

JEANNE: So what... you know well that here he didn't sell anything, he didn't see anybody... We don't have money any more, Mother, you know that too.

EUDOXIE: Oh yes, that I know! Your father spent his entire savings. But you believe that in Paris, your Modigliani will find a way to take care of you? You think the whole world is waiting for him and that he's going to make sales? That suddenly everybody is going to rush to buy his paintings! People don't care about his paintings!

JEANNE: What do you want? For him to stop painting?

EUDOXIE: That's life! Sir should face up to his responsibilities. He's a family man, now. Let him have a family man's job!

JEANNE: An accountant, like Father?

EUDOXIE: What would be wrong with that?
JEANNE: Mother, some people can't be accountants.
EUDOXIE: Anybody could be an accountant! You think your father is highly intelligent?
JEANNE: It's not a question of intelligence.
EUDOXIE: Of will then!? That man has plenty of will, to persist in painting despite everyone's opinions. Why would he lack the will to do accounts? In general, members his race are good at it…
JEANNE: Mother!
EUDOXIE: Accountant or carpenter, he has to find a job… a useful job that pays well. What is the use of a painter?
JEANNE: To… to make the world more beautiful… to make sense of life…
EUDOXIE *(astounded for a moment)*: Ah but you're right… he made you radiant, and look what he's done with your life. A great work of art!
JEANNE *(lowered eyes)*: … You have never accepted that I might be happy.
EUDOXIE: Happy…! At twenty, in this rat hole, without a penny, and with a child of unknown father!
JEANNE: You said you were in Nice to help me… You are just here to watch the unfolding disaster.
EUDOXIE: I'm not responsible for your misery, my daughter. You're the only one to blame; you were unable to keep your man, you thought you were superior to ordinary people, you believed you would be different from everyone else.

The baby cries again, EUDOXIE *takes her in her arms.*

EUDOXIE *(cradling the baby)*: Don't cry my child, my small one, my abandoned Jeanne. Your grandmother is here, now. You're not alone any more. *(Humming.)*

> *My candle is dead,*
> *I don't have a light any more,*
> *Open your door for me,*
> *For God's sake…*

ACT FOUR

In the Parisian studio, even more miserable than in the beginning.

SCENE 1

MODI and ZBO seated around a table, eating. MODI is in his bathrobe, haggard face, pallor of a spectre, his voice faded and weary.

ZBO: Do you know how many of your paintings the organisers of the exhibition took?

MODI: A thousand?

ZBO *(without noting)*: Nine! Nine paintings… of the hundred and fifty-eight on display. And fifty drawings, which sold at one shilling each!

MODI: I'm going to be Rothschild!

ZBO: Picasso has only six paintings and Matisse four.

MODI: Poor them.

ZBO: And do you know what Arnold Bennett has written in the foreword of the Exhibition's catalogue?

MODI: That I'm a genius?

ZBO *(proudly declaiming)*: "I suspect the portraits of Modigliani to be true masterpieces."

MODI *(fussy)*: He "suspects"!?
ZBO: You're never satisfied.
MODI: Suspected, and I should jump for joy?
ZBO *(after a moment, looking at the empty plate)*: Not enjoying the meal my wife cooked you?
MODI: I am, I am.
ZBO: You haven't eaten a thing.
MODI: I don't feel hungry. The Zborowska has nothing to do with it.
ZBO: You have to get back your strength. I think you've lost weight.
MODI: About ten pounds, no more.
ZBO: And how are your lungs?
MODI: Full of blood. Real fountains of it.
ZBO: You must see a doctor, Amedeo! You have to find out the cause.
MODI: Lost cause.
ZBO: It's alcohol, if I may say so – you're drinking more than before.
MODI: You have to know how to break through your boundaries.
ZBO: And as for the life you're leading... you were spotted, the day before yesterday, in the dead of night in the middle of boulevard Raspail, you were staggering...
MODI: Don't worry about that.
ZBO: What should I worry about then?
MODI: My brain.
ZBO: Your brain?
MODI: My brain is mush, Zbo. I have blurred vision, I have atrocious headaches, Zbo, like hammer blows to the

ZBO: skull. But if only that was all... I can't concentrate on painting any more. Believe me, Zbo, sickness has gone to my head.

ZBO: You're losing your mind.

MODI: That's what I'm saying.

ZBO: What does Jeanne say about it?

MODI: That she loves me. And will until death. Jeanne is a source of great comfort.

ZBO: I have to talk to her.

MODI: Don't scare her needlessly. In her condition...

ZBO: Her condition?

MODI: You noticed I have lost some weight. But you don't see anything wrong with her!?

ZBO: She is...

MODI: Pregnant. Yes, Zbo, I will be a father for the second time. And this time, it will be a son, and I will recognise him.

MODI: Let's hurry him along. Then he can see his father alive and famous. Born of a recognised father. And then...

ZBO: Then?

MODI: Later, promise to take care of my two orphans.

ZBO: Don't talk like that.

MODI: Soon I won't talk at all.

ZBO: You'll talk, you'll paint... Life goes on.

MODI: It will go on without me.

ZBO: Why are you so pessimistic?

MODI: I have told you a hundred times, my lot, we die of madness, or tuberculosis. I will have got both.

ZBO: You won't die. Dr Guillaume will save you.

MODI: How can well-meaning men lie so badly? I'm telling you that I know when the disease has reached my brain. I know what I'm saying. I saw my uncle, Amedeo, I saw my cousins. This shit drags on silently for years, doing nothing more than making you spit red, but when it decides to move on and go up to your skull, it takes you in two weeks... Well, when I die, prices will increase. This is the privilege of painters. More expensive dead than alive...

Silence. They eat. Small bites for MODI.

ZBO *(after a moment and changing his tone)*: I found a buyer for your "Zouave". He has offered me a thousand francs. We have never got that kind of money, but I'll boost the price... *(Silence.)* That doesn't seem to please you?
MODI: What doesn't?
ZBO: That I found a buyer for a thousand francs.
MODI: That's your job, isn't it?
ZBO: It's the fourth painting in a week.
MODI: The fifth is yours.
ZBO: What?
MODI: For four sold paintings, I offer you one. You deserve it.
ZBO: I'm not asking for that much.
MODI: What are you asking for then?
ZBO: Just a little gratitude.
MODI: Because you're doing your job? Do I get a bit of gratitude also?
ZBO: Oh yes! This month, I sold twelve paintings, more than the whole of last year.

MODI: I don't recognise myself.
ZBO: What do you mean?
MODI: I see myself in the mirror, you know. It looks like someone else. It surprises me each time. I'm scaring myself.
ZBO: You, scared?
MODI: You know what I see in the mirror?... I see Amedeo.
ZBO: Sorry, I don't understand.
MODI: My uncle, Amedeo. In Livorno, at the end, he was living with us. It's him I'm seeing in the mirror.
ZBO: A family resemblance, that's normal.
MODI: No, Zbo, that's not what I'm seeing in the mirror.
ZBO: What do you see, then?
MODI: Can't you guess?
ZBO: I didn't meet your uncle. I'd have liked to, mind you. Him and your mother. The way you talk about her, she seems a very good person, your mother.
MODI: She was a genius, my mother, a beauty, one of a kind. The Virgin Mary and Marie Curie. Oh, when I see Madam Eudoxie Hébuterne, I keep telling myself that's the reason why all this has happened... because I walked away from my mother.
ZBO: What happened?
MODI: My last hour, Zbo.
ZBO: Don't talk rubbish.
MODI: You know, I let you insult me, it means it's the end... And that's what I see in the mirror, my friend, the ghost of my uncle... When I was five, I was watching him, hidden behind the door, being rubbed with a massage glove in the bathroom. He was nude,

skinny as a stick, a bag of bones. He was looking at me, with his bulging eyes which terrified me, and despite the softness in his eyes, I couldn't help being scared, despite all the love I had for him. He was so skinny, a corpse with the power of speech. One day, he turned around, looked at me with his dead eyes and said: "Dedo, are you afraid of your uncle? Why stay outside the door? Come in!" I went in. "Close the door," he said, "in case your mother sees me like this, she would be frightened, my sister." I closed the door behind me. He said: "Do you know why I'm rubbing so hard with the massage glove, my Dedo?" I shook my head. He said: "It's to get rid of death. You know, surely you have heard about it, everybody says so here. I've got death in my bronchi. But I think I can make it go away. I just need to remove it, little by little. You know, death is not stronger than the Modiglianis. Nobody can kill a Modigliani. So it's not tuberculosis that will do it… By rubbing, I will remove it. But it resists, this stuff; it clings, it sticks to my skin, under my bones. Dedo, would you help me? I can't take it out of my back, so what I'm doing is useless. If I leave some, it will be back… Help me, Dedo, to snatch death away." He gave me the massage glove, turned his back on me, and asked me to climb on the stool and rub his back and shoulders hard. "Snatch away, snatch away!" he said. And me, I was rubbing as hard as I could, I was rubbing and trying to hold back my tears. He was saying, "That's good, Dedo, harder, I'm coming

Modigliani

alive again, thanks to you, Dedo, rub harder, I feel it going away. Don't be afraid to hurt me, I don't feel anything any more." I was burning my hands. And suddenly there were blood drops running down my hands and falling to the floor. He said, as he saw it, "Bravo Dedo, keep going, you are making death run. You are curing me. Rub, rub!" That's when the door opened and my mother appeared. *(He stops. A long silence.)* Zbo, don't you want to rub my back?

A short silence. JEANNE *enters in her nightgown, round belly, rubbing her eyes.*

JEANNE: Was I asleep for a long time?
MODI: A good month.
ZBO: Come eat with us, dear Jeanne. My wife prepared something, one of her Polish specialities. You'll love it.

JEANNE sits at the table.

MODI: OK, but the Zborowska forgot about drinks. How can you eat meat without wine?! I'm going down to buy a bottle.
JEANNE: At this time?
MODI: The owner of La Rotonde is serving me again. Since I have reimbursed my debt and paid cash on the nail. You see, it helps that you sell my paintings. You're clearing my debts at La Rotonde.

MODI *gets up.*

JEANNE: You can't go out like that...
MODI: There's a nice breeze, it'll make me feel better. That's how they treat people like us. Fresh air, large sanatoriums.
JEANNE: Léopold, do something!
MODI: Ah no, Zbo, don't move or you will be agreeing to rub my back too!... Don't worry, Jeanne, I'll be back in two minutes with a good bottle.

He exits with an unsteady walk.

SCENE 2

JEANNE and ZBO around the table.
JEANNE devours her food.

ZBO: It's good you came back.
JEANNE: I'm not so sure.
ZBO: He needs you. You... and a doctor.
JEANNE: He wouldn't listen... At night, with what he spits, I fill buckets of blood... He says it will pass, that we just have to wait. We'll go to Livorno to see his mother and there, he'll regain his health. We're just short of the money for the journey.
ZBO: Very soon, I assure you. They are talking about him among all the art dealers. They come here to see his paintings. And with the end of the war, people are buying again. The London Exhibition will be a triumph, his consecration. I'm even dreaming about an

article in *The Burlington Magazine*. In three months, I assure you, you'll be able to go to Italy.

JEANNE *(smiling)*: May God hear you! You know we're going to get married. He promised me. Léopold, I'm going to be a lady before the birth of the child. Then, we'll take Jeanne from her nanny and we'll leave for Livorno. We'll be a family, a large family. And you, you will be godfather to my second daughter, I'm sure it's a girl. That's who I am, I make girls. Do you accept?

ZBO: With pleasure!

JEANNE: Will you spoil her?

ZBO: With all the gold in the world.

JEANNE: It's nice to spoil her. Girls can never be too spoiled. You'll come and see her, won't you? Dedo told me that in Livorno, we'll live in a palace, a big palace of marble. He'll paint frescos over our bed, frescos more beautiful than Raphael's… It will be worth all these sacrifices, won't it?

ZBO: Of course.

JEANNE: You just need to be confident. But I always knew that one day, we'd be happy. There's no reason why not, is there?

ZBO: None.

JEANNE: My mother tells me sometimes that we are cursed.

ZBO: Your mother is sometimes excessive.

JEANNE: We're not cursed, are we?

ZBO: Curses don't exist.

JEANNE: You know, in Livorno, in our palace, you'll choose your room. Here, we're not very good hosts.

ZBO: I'm at home here.
JEANNE: But there... Dedo says he will build the foundations himself. He knows what to do with stone, doesn't he?
ZBO: A great sculptor.
JEANNE: There will still be a room for my mother. Insults don't bother me.
ZBO: You know how to forgive. You're a pure soul, Jeanne.
JEANNE: That's not what my mother says, but I forgive her, she's worried... I know what it is now, the worry of a mother.
ZBO: Soon, nobody'll have to worry.
JEANNE (*a silence. She eats.*): Tell me, please, would you go and see if Dedo has found his way back? La Rotonde is only next door, but in his state...

ZBO gets up.

ZBO: I'll go immediately.
JEANNE: You're our saviour, Léopold.

SCENE 3

JEANNE alone, softly dancing, caressing her belly.

JEANNE: We are going to be happy, my baby. Your father is going to become famous. After, we'll be rich. We'll take your sister back from her nanny. And you, I will never leave you with someone else. I will feed you. It shouldn't be so complicated when you have enough to eat. We'll leave for Livorno. Your father will speak to you in Italian, and me, in French, you'll speak all languages. Oh you'll have a magnificent room, a marble cradle, goose down mattress. Apparently that exists. Poor geese. I will give you your bath in our swimming pool. And you'll drink your soup with a silver spoon. We will be happy, my daughter. In the evening, we will have our dinner near a big fireplace. And then Amedeo will fall asleep on my shoulder. Never again will he get the idea to go out to bars, find other women. I will be the one, the only, his love and joy, we'll surround him, the three of us. He'll receive so much affection and tenderness that life will look like paradise on earth for him. He will be covered in glory and we, we'll surround him with our kisses, we'll keep him warm, and he'll be happy, my love, my soul. He won't need drink any more. You heard what Léopold said, curses don't exist. He knows what he is talking about; Mr Zborowski, he's come a long way, he's seen the world.

We hear noises coming from the stairs, something like a body being dragged. ZBO *appears, he supports* MODI *by the shoulder.* JEANNE *goes to help them.*

ZBO: No, don't tire yourself, not in your state!
JEANNE: Where did you find him, in the bar!?
ZBO: If only, but no! He hadn't even crossed the road; he was in front of the building, on the asphalt, semi-conscious and shivering.

JEANNE: He has to lie down… in the room.

They walk towards the room.

ZBO: He needs a doctor.
JEANNE: No, no, he doesn't want that. That would be a betrayal to him, a betrayal of his will. It will pass. We just need to wait. He's strong; nothing keeps him down, nothing can sap his strength.

SCENE 4

ZBO and JEANNE in the studio. JEANNE now has a nine-month size belly. ZBO holds the newspaper in his hands. The door to the bedroom is closed.

ZBO: How is he?
JEANNE: He will be fine.
ZBO: Is he sleeping?
JEANNE: He's resting.
ZBO: May I see him?
JEANNE: I'll ask him.

She opens the door to the bedroom and stays a moment inside. ZBO flicks restlessly through his newspaper and finds the desired page. JEANNE comes back still looking sad and leaving the door open. She stands at the door.

JEANNE: He's not feeling well.

ZBO: What I'm going to tell him will get him back on his feet; he'll jump out of bed when he hears the news.

JEANNE *(turning to the room)*: Can you listen, Dedo? *(After a while, turning to* ZBO.*)* He's nodding that he can hear.

ZBO *(speaking a bit louder)*: Amedeo, here we are, glory is assured! You won't believe it, you have an article in... wait for it, in *The Burlington Magazine*. Can you hear me, Amedeo, *The Burlington Magazine?*

JEANNE *(turning her head alternately to the room and to* ZBO*)*: He's nodding yes.

ZBO: And does he look happy?

JEANNE: He's over the moon.

ZBO *(for Jeanne)* Imagine, *The Burlington Magazine*, the most prestigious art magazine in Europe – I should say – in the world! *(Louder.)* A full page, Amedeo, a page in the *Burlington*!

JEANNE *(in the middle between both)*: He's still smiling. Come in. I haven't seen this happy look on his face for weeks.

ZBO *(loud)*: And guess who signed the article? Roger Fry, the great English critic, the man who's running the show in galleries, the friend of Kahnweiler. *(For Jeanne.)* Can he hear?

JEANNE: He's enjoying it!

ZBO *(grabbing the newspaper with two hands and his eyes on the article)*: Listen to this Amedeo, I want to read. (For Jeanne.) How is he?

JEANNE: Both eyes wide open. Read, Léopold!

ZBO *(with a strong voice, softer when he talks to Jeanne)*: I start. "Modigliani's approach to relief is that of a sculptor." A sculptor, Amedeo... It's written here!

JEANNE: He agrees.

ZBO: I will continue! "Which doesn't mean the colour is wrong: quite the reverse, it's precisely because he considers it as a means to amplify his line that the problem is solved. His method is the opposite of Cézanne's...!" *(To Jeanne.)* How is he?

JEANNE: He's gloating!

ZBO: He hasn't heard anything yet! "What prevents his colour from being dull or monotonous is precisely what prevents his tone being too mechanically exact, which means a powerful sense – here again, like a sculptor's – of surface quality!"

JEANNE: He's in heaven!

ZBO: "His nearly exaggerated sensitivity plays around each surface particle with infinite variations of treatment, nearly imperceptible, and with tiny nuances of colour."

JEANNE: Continue!

ZBO: "In a word, an immense artist is born, an equal to Picasso and Matisse!"

JEANNE: Repeat, repeat!

ZBO: "In a word..."

JEANNE: No, just the end!

ZBO: "... an equal to Picasso and Matisse!"

JEANNE *(approaching Léopold)*: Come here, Léopold, come, I want to kiss you.

ZBO *(approaching her)*: Oh, I've got nothing to do with it!

JEANNE *(she kisses him on his cheeks, then faces him)*: We won, Léopold, we won! Oh, it was well worth the effort.

ZBO: All our efforts.

JEANNE *(speaking in a sobbing, amplifying voice)*: Those nights without sleep, those evenings waiting.

ZBO: All the nights in the world.

JEANNE: And those wild mornings, when he'd drunk too much.

ZBO: All the mornings in the world.

JEANNE: Those months of starvation. Those shivering winters.

ZBO: It's over, now.

JEANNE: Over, behind us. Oh, they recognised him, the greatest, the best of them.

ZBO: Equal to Picasso.

JEANNE: We, we knew it.

ZBO: Everybody will know it! *The Burlington Magazine*, Jeanne!

JEANNE: Oh, what a day, Léopold!

ZBO: We have waited a long time for this day.

JEANNE: It wasn't all for nothing, was it?

ZBO: Who'd dare say that? Nobody now!

JEANNE goes back to the door of the room.

JEANNE: My love, did you hear? *(Turning to ZBO.)* He's closed his eyes.

ZBO: Too much emotion probably.

JEANNE *(towards the room)*: Sleep, my love, my life force, my soul… *(Towards ZBO.)* He's so pale. We should perhaps call…

ZBO: After this news, he'll accept, for sure. He'll want to look after himself, show he's brave, ready to carry on...

JEANNE *(towards* MODI*)*: My love?

ZBO: His work.

JEANNE *(in a heartbreaking cry and going into the room)*: My love!?... *(From inside.)* Léopold! Come, come! Quickly!

> ZBO *rushes into the room.*

JEANNE *(from the room, in a sob)*: My love, my soul... Léopold, call the doctor, an ambulance, quick...

> ZBO *comes out the door, running.*
> *Crosses the stage and exits.*

JEANNE *(from the room, in a sob)*: My friend, my life...

SCENE 5

At the back of the stage, an immense luminous photographic landscape showing the hills of Tuscany in the distance. A house in the foreground. A sort of patio. A table, two chairs. A big cradle nearby. ZBO *and an old lady, Amedeo's mother,* EUGÉNIE MODIGLIANI, *seated around the table with cups of coffee in front of them.*

EUGÉNIE: So it wasn't true, all that I was told?

ZBO: Lies, Madam Modigliani.
EUGÉNIE: That he was drinking?
ZBO: Less than me.
EUGÉNIE: Newspapers, even here, the *Stampa* said he was always drunk, dead drunk in Montmartre, the shame of Italy.
ZBO: You believe the newspapers?
EUGÉNIE: And drugs. I have been told about hashish.
ZBO: Malicious people.
EUGÉNIE: That he was taking opium.
ZBO: Jealous people!
EUGÉNIE: What made me smile was when I was told that women were attracted to him. This was right, wasn't it, Mr Zborowski?
ZBO: The absolute truth, Madam. Not one could resist him!
EUGÉNIE: He was so beautiful, so strong.
ZBO: Charm incarnate.
EUGÉNIE: Did you know him well?
ZBO: Better than anyone else.
EUGÉNIE: You were his friend?
ZBO: I admired him too much to be his friend.
EUGÉNIE: You admired... my son?
ZBO: Your son is admirable, Madam. Your son is a giant; a Raphael, a Caravaggio.
EUGÉNIE: I didn't realise...
ZBO: Amedeo is a genius.
EUGÉNIE: Was, you mean.
ZBO: Me, I have the feeling he's still talking to me.
EUGÉNIE: I saw him so little these last few years.
ZBO: He was thinking only of you.

EUGÉNIE: Why didn't he come? We'd have been happy, here. I'd have taken care of him. I'd have saved him.
ZBO: He was planning to come, with Jeanne.
EUGÉNIE: How was she, his wife?
ZBO: An angel, Madam, an angel.
EUGÉNIE: Did she love him?
ZBO: Like no one else.
EUGÉNIE: And he, he loved her?
ZBO: More than any other woman.
EUGÉNIE: Why did she join him, like that, so quickly, so horribly?
ZBO: She couldn't wait. To live a day without him was not living.
EUGÉNIE: She should have waited. To end it like that, so tragically. To throw herself from a building, that baby in her belly. I would have raised her child.
ZBO: You have her first girl. And her girl is so beautiful.
EUGÉNIE: No, it's too terrible.
ZBO: Yes, terrible.
EUGÉNIE: What does one do to deserve this? Nobody deserves this...

Cries coming from the big cradle. EUGÉNIE *goes to take the child – a two year old girl – in her arms, cradles her.*

EUGÉNIE: She's got Dedo's eyes, hasn't she?
ZBO: And her mother's smile.
EUGÉNIE: Jeanne, my Gionova, we'll teach you to live, here. Me, I'll look after you and when I'm not there any more, it will be my daughter Margherita who'll take

care of you. You'll live, my little girl... *(Humming a nursery rhyme.)*

Din don Din don,
La campana di fra' Simon,
Eran due che la sonavan,
Pane vin i' domandavan

The child stops crying.

EUGÉNIE *(resuming and addressing the child)*: You, we won't let you leave. You'll stay here. *(Towards* ZBO.*)* It wouldn't do any good to leave, would it, Mr Zborowski?

ZBO: No. No good.

EUGÉNIE *continues to cradle her little girl, humming.*

CURTAIN